LIFE CYCLE OF A SALMON

by Noah Leatherland

Minneapolis, Minnesota

Credits
All images are courtesy of Shutterstock.com, unless otherwise specified. With thanks to Getty Images, Thinkstock Photo, and iStockphoto. Cover – Erik Lam, Semenaka_Maria. Recurring images – Mubeen Arif, uiliaaa, YummyBuum, tanyaya, WinWinFolly, Sasi Gallery, Foxy Fox, Borodatch. 2 – jack perks, slowmotiongli. 4–5 – Dernkadel, sirtravelalot, Pixel-Shot, Africa Studio, fizkes, LightField Studios. 6–7 – slowmotiongli, Andrei Armiagov. 8–9 – Ronnie Chua, Konstantin Baidin. 10–11 – Konstantin Baidin, OpenCage, CC BY-SA 2.5 via Wikimedia Commons. 12–13 – yamaoyaji, Peter Steenstra at the Green Lake National Fish Hatchery, Public domain, via Wikimedia Commons. 14–15 – jack perks, Eran Hakim, Arthur Campbell. 16–17 – Konstantin Novikov, MotionPixxle Studio, Dietrich Leppert. 18–19 – Sekar B, Jennifer Nicole Buchanan, Eduardo Baena. 20–21 – AndreAnita, Lynn Batchelor- Browning, Russ Heinl, Romix Image. 22–23 – Konstantin Baidin, yamaoyaji, jack perks, Krasowit, Aristokrates, Peter Steenstra at the Green Lake National Fish Hatchery, Public domain, via Wikimedia Commons.

Bearport Publishing Company Product Development Team
Publisher: Jen Jenson; Director of Product Development: Spencer Brinker; Managing Editor: Allison Juda; Editor: Cole Nelson; Associate Editor: Naomi Reich; Associate Editor: Tiana Tran; Designer: Kim Jones; Designer: Kayla Eggert; Designer: Steve Scheluchin; Production Specialist: Owen Hamlin

Library of Congress Cataloging-in-Publication Data is available at www.loc.gov or upon request from the publisher.

ISBN: 979-8-89577-017-7 (hardcover)
ISBN: 979-8-89577-448-9 (paperback)
ISBN: 979-8-89577-134-1 (ebook)

© 2026 BookLife Publishing
This edition is published by arrangement with BookLife Publishing.

North American adaptations © 2026 Bearport Publishing Company. All rights reserved. No part of this publication may be reproduced in whole or in part, stored in any retrieval system, or transmitted in any form or by any means, electronic, mechanical, photocopying, recording, or otherwise, without written permission from the publisher. Bearport Publishing is a division of FlutterBee Education Group.

For more information, write to Bearport Publishing, 5357 Penn Avenue South, Minneapolis, MN 55419.

Contents

What Is a Life Cycle?. 4
Salmon on the Farm 6
Laying Eggs 8
Alevins 10
Fry and Parr 12
Saltwater Smolts 14
All Grown Up 16
The Journey of a Salmon. . . . 18
The End of Life. 20
Life Cycle of a Salmon 22
Glossary 24
Index 24

WHAT IS A LIFE CYCLE?

All living things go through different stages of life. We come into the world and grow over time. Eventually, we die. This is the life cycle.

BABY

TODDLER

CHILD

As humans, we start life as babies. We grow into toddlers and children. Then, we become teenagers. Finally, we are adults and get even older. We may have babies of our own, and then the cycle begins again.

SALMON ON THE FARM

Some salmon are wild, while others live on farms. Wild salmon start life in **freshwater** rivers, swim to the ocean, and then go back to the rivers to have young. Farmers create this life cycle for salmon on the farm.

There are about eight different kinds of salmon.

Fish farming is sometimes called aquaculture (AH-kwa-*kuhl*-chur).

A SALMON FARM

Fish farms are different from other farms. They are made up of large **tanks**, cages, and nets in rivers and seas. Salmon farms often have thousands of fish. Farmers raise these animals for their meat.

LAYING EGGS

Salmon start out as eggs in rivers. **Female** salmon dig nests, called redds, where they lay thousands of eggs.

SALMON EGGS

When salmon lay eggs, it is called spawning.

Only eggs that have been **fertilized** will grow into salmon. Farmers often help fertilize the eggs on farms. Then, they collect the eggs in trays filled with water.

ALEVINS

After about six weeks, the eggs **hatch**. The baby salmon are called alevins (AH-luh-vinz). These little fish have the yolks of their eggs stuck to them. The **nutrients** in the yolks help alevins grow.

YOLK

Alevins can grow to be about 1 inch (2.5 cm) long.

Farmers put the alevins in small freshwater tanks that have sand and **gravel** at the bottom. The little fish bury themselves in the gravel until their yolks are gone.

FRY AND PARR

Once out of the gravel, the little fish are called fry. Young fry swim to the surface of the water and take a gulp of air. This helps them float and swim.

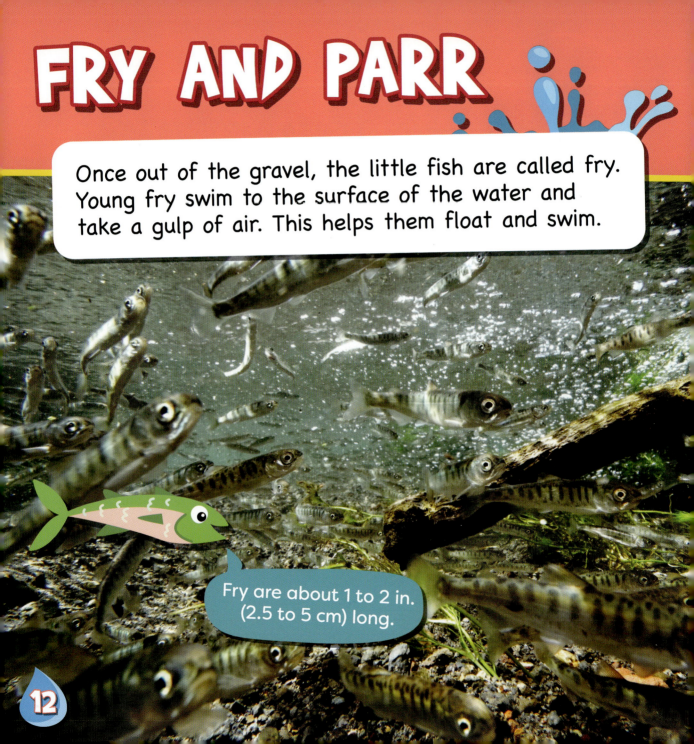

Fry are about 1 to 2 in. (2.5 to 5 cm) long.

Salmon parr are sometimes called fingerlings because they are about as long as a finger.

Then, the farmers move the fry into larger freshwater tanks. The young fish eat mostly small bugs and fish eggs. After about a year, the fish are called parr.

SALTWATER SMOLTS

When the parr have grown big enough, their bodies change so they can live in salt water. They also turn a silvery color. At this stage, the fish are called smolts.

Smolts eat other small fish.

A WELL BOAT

It is time for the salmon to live in the ocean. Some farmers use special boats, called well boats, to move the smolts to sea cages. The fish live and grow in these cages.

15

ALL GROWN UP

Some types of salmon grow faster than others. A few become adults after only a year swimming in the sea cages. Others take as long as eight years to become fully grown.

An adult salmon can weigh up to 80 pounds (40 kg).

As adults, the salmon are able to have their own young. Salmon that have young are called brood stock.

THE JOURNEY OF A SALMON

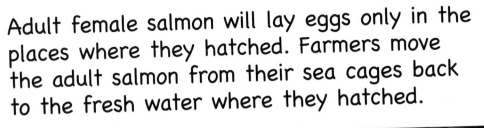

Adult female salmon will lay eggs only in the places where they hatched. Farmers move the adult salmon from their sea cages back to the fresh water where they hatched.

Salmon stop eating when they return to fresh water.

Many kinds of salmon change shape and color before they have young. Some salmon get bright red bodies with green heads. Others grow a large bump on their backs.

THE END OF LIFE

Salmon have many natural **predators**, including bears, seals, and other fish. Most farmers keep their salmon safe in cages that are covered with nets.

A BEAR

A SEAL

Salmon can live for about 13 years. However, most farm salmon don't live this long since they are raised for their meat.

LIFE CYCLE OF A SALMON

A salmon begins its life as an egg. An alevin hatches and grows. It quickly becomes a fry, then a parr, and soon it grows into a smolt. Eventually, it becomes an adult.

During its life, a salmon may lay eggs of its own. The salmon will die, but the new fish live on and make even more salmon. This keeps the life cycle going!

Glossary

female a salmon that can lay eggs

fertilized made able to grow into a baby animal

freshwater having to do with water that does not have salt

gravel small, crushed rocks

hatch to break out of an egg

nutrients substances plants and animals need to grow and stay healthy

predators animals that hunt and eat other animals

tanks large containers for holding liquids

Index

alevins 10-11, 22
eggs 8-10, 13, 18, 22-23
farmer 6-7, 9, 11, 13, 15, 18, 20
net 7, 20
parr 12-14, 22
predators 20
rivers 6-8
smolts 14-15, 22
well boats 15
yolks 10-11